I'm Retired...Now What?

I'm Retired...Now What?

• • •

99 "Adventures" To Fulfill During Retirement

Kyle A Sadler, AIF®, CRC®

ISBN-13: 9780692468180
ISBN-10: 0692468188
Library of Congress Control Number: 2015909685
Kyle A. Sadler, Humble, TX

Dedication

First, to the One who dedicated His life for me.

Next, to Denise, Kyli, and Zoe, the ones who are my daily motivation.

And, of course, to my clients and all the retirees whom I have worked with and will assist with this book.

Table of Contents

Foreword

Throughout the sixteen years I've been a financial advisor, years, my primary client base has been retirees. Over that time period, I have found a commonality among those who are happy, long-lived, and productive throughout their retirement. That commonality boils down to staying active. Unless you are waiting to greet a slow and painful death, the key to longevity is keeping the body and mind in shape through constant activity. This is not to say that you should seek strenuous and exhausting activities, but you need to keep the momentum pushing forward to avoid an early grave.

This book is a collection of ideas that I refer to as adventures. I call them adventures for two primary reasons. Of course the first that comes to my mind is that learning something new can appear to be an adventure in itself. New technology, a new craft, or even a reconnection with something or someone from your past can be an adventure. The second is the advice I give to all: the journey through retirement should be your adventure, not a routine.

Some adventures are singular and meant to be pursued over the long term, while others should be incorporated together as part of multiple ideas for added adventure and entertainment. In fact, the content of these adventures may be pursued at any pace you feel is sufficient for your entertainment and in any order *you* may choose. Start from the back, middle, or anywhere you desire within this book; choose your own adventure.

As any world-renowned and competent author (hey, I can dream!) would, I did some extensive research. This research included talking to a one-hundred-year-old man, remembering what my grandmother told me when I was younger, and stealing ideas from people who had already done more research than I have done to compile the ideas in this book. Therefore, if you think any of these ideas are corny or farfetched, it's because they came from someone else. However, if you exclaim, "*Wow! That's a really cool and smart idea*," I thought of it.

This book is intended to go beyond the bounds of planning to be a checkout person at Walmart to occupy your time during retirement.

The main point is that I don't want to hear that you're bored; there's more than enough to do! And once you do everything in this book, then think of more. Remember, life is an adventure, so enjoy it!

—Kyle A. Sadler

I

Physical Pursuits

We've probably all heard the saying, "A body in motion stays in motion."

One of the keys to longevity is maintaining and increasing mental and physical acuteness and flexibility. Of course, the obvious theme in this section is exercise. However, a retiree needs to explore alternatives to a traditional workout due to overexposure to the monotony of the workout, which can kill his or her motivation. As the old saying goes, "A rolling stone gathers no moss."

I recognize that every reader has his or her own physical limitations, and I would be negligent if I told you otherwise. However, don't let your mental limitations override your physical. There will be some adventures about which your mind will say, "I can't do that," but your body is saying, "I can still do that." Listen to your body (and doctor). Remember, this is more about the journey and less about overexerting yourself. People might hear me say that the recliner may seem tempting, but I call it "The Death Chair"; however, disobeying your doctor is not a wise option.

The following examples contain some productive means for a retiree to maintain and increase his or her physical fitness.

1
Moving to the Country

Ah, the fresh, quiet, and still country air! What better way to get exercise than to enjoy Mother Nature at her best. The spring-time flowers whiffed in the meadows, the strolls taken along the stream, the painted sunsets of the Texas Hill Country—life is fulfilled in the enjoyment of natural beauty. Moving to the country may be the answer.

There is often this misconception that "life on the farm is kinda laid back." On the contrary, living in the country involves more physical labor and upkeep than living in the city ever could. Although physical fitness can be achieved through the daily chores of working wherever you live, just remember that the more land there is, the more responsibility that you'll assume. And if animals are added into the mix, even more time and physical activity will be required.

An additional warning, don't overlook the limitations that come with age. The average retiree is age sixtyish. At this age, physical activity is still maintainable, but the reality is that as your age increases, physical limitations will likely occur. Therefore, make the decision to move to the country with caution, because although the peace and tranquility may seem alluring, there may be some physical limits that come to you in the future.

2
Moving to the City

On the other hand, moving to the city can be a different kind of adventure. For retirees who have lived in the country or small communities, city life can add a new dynamic. In a larger town (population: fifty thousand plus), there are more activities available for retirees. There are also more places to explore. It's funny to see how many people travel the world to explore new destinations but fail to explore the reason why visitors come to their town.

3
Remodeling Your House

There is an old saying: "If you want to test your marriage, build a house." Well, to remodel a house is not far off. However, if you go into the remodeling project with the anticipation of it being fun, and not a chore or job, then the perspective will change, and it might make the venture something that can be enjoyed. Also, remodeling a house can be a money-making experience for those who are interested in real-estate rental or "flipping" a house. However, if this is to become a money-making experience, you'll need to surround yourself with honest and knowledgeable individuals to provide guidance. Remember, those who speak the most about how honest and knowledgeable they are often are the ones who know the least and may not have your best interests at heart.

4
Moving to a Different City Once a Year

It's a given that moving is a strenuous exercise. Packing boxes, moving them, loading furniture—I start sweating just thinking about the moving process. People always say, "I'll never move again," based on the sheer exhaustion from their move; however, here is a new twist to the idea: Retirees often talk about downsizing when it comes to their house since they are now "empty nesters." (Sometimes "empty nesters" want to make sure they remain that way by not having spare bedrooms.)

Moving to a different city once a year is a different twist on taking summer trips in an RV or, on the flip side, settling down in a retirement community where the retiree plans to live out the rest of his or her days. To make this feasibly possible, the retiree would simply downsize their belongings (you can't take them with you anyway) and rent an apartment or a house for one year each year. This way, the retiree can explore the area around where they live, yet not have any ties to a mortgage or "stuff." If done correctly, this method is less expensive than traveling/vacationing to various locations.

5
Conquering a Fear

They say that the best way to conquer a fear is to face it. How adventurous would it be to face your biggest fear by placing it right in front of yourself? What is your phobia? Snakes? Then

visit a snake farm (and keep going until you lose that fear). Afraid of heights? Go skydiving! President George H. W. Bush did it on his eighty-fifth birthday, so don't make the excuse that you are too old! Have multiple fears? Well, face them all. People spend a lifetime avoiding their fears, but you're retired now and you have already faced the biggest challenges in life through your adulthood. Think of the often-cited words, "The only thing we have to fear is fear itself."

6
Setting a World Record

This next idea could have been classified under multiple headings; however, it ended up in the "Physical Pursuits" chapter. What's a better way for a retiree to stay busy than to plan and execute setting a world record? World records are not all physical activities; in fact, the majority of the records in the *Guinness Book of World Records* require no physical activity at all. Take, for example, the record for "Largest Gathering of People Dressed as Dogs," which is 264. My challenge to you could be to round up at least 265 people and beat it. What about joining the "Largest Gathering of Elvis Impersonators" in Las Vegas next time they challenge the world record?

Do you want something not as ridiculous and a little more challenging? How about "Most Spoons Balanced on the Face"? Retirees have the one commodity that most people don't, and that is time! Be creative, but most of all, have fun. The world's largest ball of twine didn't happen overnight. So remember, every world record starts with the phrase "I can do that!"

A little afterthought and a goal to strive for—the oldest gymnast is eighty-six years old. There's a goal: surpass her age as a gymnast.

7
Mining for Gems

I actually thought of this idea right after my family and I came back from vacation. Part of our vacation this year was to stop at the Crater of Diamonds State Park in Arkansas. A great retirement trip is to travel to a place where you can mine for gems. There are areas open all over the world in which the general public can mine legally. This isn't to get rich; it's all about discovery. My whole goal in Arkansas was to find a diamond. It didn't matter how big or small. Unfortunately, I didn't find one, but the funny part is that a twelve-year-old kid found an over-five-carat diamond in the same spot the next day. I think I was more excited that he found it than I would've been if I had. How fun is finding a buried treasure!

I just would like to throw out a few words of caution with regards to digging for gems. There are only a select few state and national parks in the United States that allow for individuals to dig and remove these items. Please check with the ranger station at the park if you are unsure of the rules.

Here is a small list of places where you can mine for gems (and gold):

- Crater of Diamonds State Park in Murfreesboro, AR (diamonds)
  craterofdiamondsstatepark.com
- Gem Mountain in Phillipsburg, MT (sapphires)
  gemmountainmt.com
- Herkimer Diamond Mines in Herkimer, NY (double-terminated quartz crystals)
  herkimerdiamond.com
- Royal Peacock Mine in Virgin Valley, NV (black fire opals)
  royalpeacock.com

- Cherokee Ruby Mine in Franklin, NC (rubies, sapphires, garnets, and moonstones)
    cherokeerubymine.com
- Emerald Hollow Mine in Hiddenite, NC (emeralds)
    hiddenitegems.com
- Rockhand State Park in Deming, NM (geodes)
    emnrd.state.nm.us
- Roaring Camp Mining in Pine Grove, CA (gold)
    roaringcampgold.com

8
Fossil and Artifact Hunting

The Earth is filled with many mysterious and really cool things. Me personally, I think fossils and artifacts are really cool. So cool that since finding my first ammonite fossil at my deer lease in West Texas, I frequent there to hunt for fossils more than I do to hunt for deer.

To expand more on hunting for fossils, while out hunting one day, I stumbled across a "cave" in the side of a hill. As I investigated it more, I discovered that it was an old Indian campsite. I uncovered some spearheads and some utensils.

Fossil and artifact hunting is another adventurous idea that you can enjoy during your retirement. While traveling, locate areas that allow for fossil and/or artifact digging.

As with mining for gems, please make sure that permission has been granted from the landowner when digging or hunting on private property. Landowners can be very funny about their property. In the beginning it may seem like they are not interested, however, once a discovery is made, they become very interested and possessive.

Also, although there are a few state and national parks that allow you to dig for and keep gems, I am not aware of any that allow you to keep fossils or other artifacts.

9
Exercising Daily

Now it's time for the most obvious under the "physical" category: exercise. There is probably not a doctor out there who would argue that daily exercise is not important to a long and healthy life. As a retiree, physical limitation may inhibit your level of exercise. However, there are many low-impact exercise programs available. Local YMCAs and other gyms have programs specially designed for less exertion. Water aerobics is very popular. Having a gym membership is not always required; there are also many libraries—yes, libraries—out there that have exercise programs available.

Additionally, tai chi is a low-impact martial art. I have possessed interest and participated in martial arts for a long period of time. As of this writing, I still participate in kung fu. I can't stress enough to retirees (and nonretirees) how beneficial tai chi really is, not just for the exercise benefits but for the total mind, body, and spirit improvement. Although tai chi may be a form of self-defense, the greatest aspect is the fact that it is a low-impact and slow-paced exercise. For senior adults, the most important elements in tai chi are the breathing, movement, and awareness exercises, as well as meditation, which I will go on to discuss.

While on a mission trip in China, I noticed that a large majority of senior adults would congregate in parks and practice tai chi together. At my own kung fu studio, probably 30 percent of the total enrolled students are senior adults, and let me tell you, they all love it!

The purpose of partaking in various exercise programs is to relieve daily stresses, increase general health, develop a structured daily regimen, and provide an active lifestyle long into retirement. Exercise is often overlooked because of "aches and pains." However, physicians who care for the elderly will always prescribe a daily dose of exercise.

10
Hiking Nature Trails

Cities, counties, improvement districts, and so forth spend millions of dollars developing hiking/walking trails. A good adventure would be to hike every nature trail within a two-hour radius. First, because it will be great exercise and keep you active; second, it's always nice to see the developments in public and private parks. Fresh air, new scenery, healthy exercise, low cost, what's not to like? And while discovering a great new park can be fun, why not share your discovery? We will discuss writing a blog later. There are thousands of trails out there and millions of things to see. Hike them, walk them, and then write about them. I bet there are other retirees just waiting to find out more.

My action plan to incorporate this in my daily life is:

_____

_____

_____

_____

_____

_____

_____

_____

_____

_____

_____

_____

II

Crafts and Hobbies

I enjoy the fact that by writing a book, I get to immortalize someone when I quote them. My grandmother once told me, "Find something you love to do, and do it for the rest of your life." This was during a conversation about finding a job; however, it relates to this section. When it comes to crafts and hobbies, we don't choose them and continue to expend our time, energy, and sometimes an overindulgence of focus on one of these activities just to pass time. No, we do it for the passion and enjoyment a craft or hobby brings to our life.

Happy retirees pursue activities that interest them. However, unhappy retirees pursue activities out of obligation or a preconceived notion that they must do it. Phil Robertson is absolutely correct when giving advice to retirees: you must find things that make you "happy, happy, happy" if you want to reach or exceed life expectancy. What is your passion? What makes you happy? OK, now do a lot more of it!

11
Gardening

Maybe you've always had a knack for gardening, or at least you've enjoyed the fact that you like working out in the garden. Now is your chance to explore your green-thumb potential. If you want to expand your knowledge, you could always join up with the Master Gardener program through a 4-H office. You don't have to already be a Master Gardener to join, but be careful, you may enjoy it so much that you become one inadvertently. Come on, who doesn't enjoy a quiet afternoon in the shade, planting and enjoying the outdoors? Golly jeepers, even Mr. Wilson from *Dennis the Menace* always enjoyed gardening...even with Dennis around.

Also, if you took the advice to move to the country, break out the tractor and plow some rows...well, at least pull out the tiller or try some square-foot gardening if acreage is not available. What to plant? If you like color, flowers. If you like vegetables, vegetables. If you don't like bugs, plant both. Flowers attracts bugs that will eat the vegetable-eating bugs (just a hint to start you off). Plant too much? Take the surplus to the farmers market. You may just make a little money, but the greatest part is you get to meet a lot of interesting people!

12
Focusing on Your Current Hobby

A lot of what I have discussed in this book has been about starting new adventures; however, not everything is about newness. How about if you focus on your current hobby? Maybe you have always enjoyed a hobby but have never had the time to pursue it as much as you have wanted to—now's your chance! Take advantage of the fact that you don't have to be anywhere tomorrow because you are retired. Don't delay—get started and enjoy what makes you happy!

13
Starting a New Hobby

After reading the previous adventure, you may be thinking, "But I don't have a hobby!" If you don't, start a new hobby today. Whether it's stamp collecting, painting, ping-pong...do whatever piques your interest. Don't see how one hobby can keep you busy? Start two, three, or four hobbies, or however many you can handle at one time. For ideas for a list of hobbies, just google "list of hobbies" and see if anything piques your interest.

14
Knitting, Crocheting, Quilting, and Needlepoint

For the next few ideas for adventures, you may think, "This would fall under the idea of hobbies." However, the defining difference I would like to point out is that hobbies are done for fun and not for money. The remaining ideas in this section are adventures that can be converted from being just a hobby to something that creates supplemental income. "Wait a second," you might say. "You mean to tell me that I can get paid to have some fun?" Absolutely! Who says you can't make any money doing something that you love to do?

Even though I have absolutely no clue about the activity, I have heard that if you knit, crochet, quilt, and/or do needle-point, your time will definitely be occupied. Although for my generation these skills are in danger of becoming a lost art, there are still many talented devotes of them, some of whom may be happy to teach a beginner. While I know nothing about how to quilt, what I do know is that when I'm watching a movie, I love to snuggle under the quilt my wife's grandmother made.

I have heard that you can also sell such items at arts and crafts fairs and that there are groups and clubs all over the nation where fellow crafters get together to work and socialize.

15
Woodworking

This next adventure is a topic I get to brag about to my dad. Although he will never admit it, Dad has always been good at woodworking, and he often refinishes furniture and builds items made of wood. This is an adventure that is broad but can be done at any time and will never go out of style. Whether you are good at refinishing or you are good at construction, woodworking is a craft that almost everyone can appreciate.

16
Golfing

Of course you were expecting this next adventure in a book for retirees; however, it almost didn't make it in here. Let's call this the ninety-ninth adventure. The reason I say this is because I could only think of ninety-eight adventures and was short one. This adventure is the ever-present sport of playing golf when you retire. "This is blasphemy!" you say. "How can he speak lowly about such a great game?" The reason I speak this way regarding golf is because most retirees feel that it's the "thing to do" when you retire. However, I have noticed over the years that most of the people on the golf course are bored. They get excited about getting a particular tee time and then complain about the group in front of them and the group behind them. They drink nonstop while out on the course. And then, at the end of the day, when they are asked, "How was your day?" the typical response is, "It beat a day of work." I am completely serious when I say this: retirees who spend three or more days a week playing golf are usually bored and feel that they must do this because they are retired. Subvert the norm! Find another adventure. Make yourself so busy that when you play golf once a month, you are telling your other three partners all the adventures you have been doing. Watch your golfing chums eyes light up with interest and the questions begin about how they can get in on the action.

17
Beach Combing

Most of us have combed the beach while on vacation, but here's a challenge: beach combing in all coastal states. Yep, once again, I am combining multiple adventures to maximize the fun element. Remember walking up and down the shorelines as a kid looking for "treasures"? You probably will not discover a long lost pirate chest of gold, but a beautiful shell or a piece of unique driftwood aren't out of the question; or you could collect a bottle of sand from each beach you visit. Imagine an ocean breeze, waves gently lapping the shore, the blue of the sky meeting the water, you get the picture. Not even the greatest of artists can paint the moments you will experience while on this peaceful adventure.

18
Metal Detecting

Metal detecting can sometimes be a subset of the previous adventure, but not everybody loses a diamond earring at the beach. However, there were many great battles fought throughout the nation that have left behind a multitude of historical artifacts. Areas throughout the United States hosted Native American conflicts, the War for Independence, and the Civil War. Most of the time, locating historical artifacts is achieved through metal detecting. However, I have read so many accounts of bank and stage-coach robbers burying their loot, and it has never been recovered. Someone's got to find it. Also, my dad lost his gold wedding band in the garden at our old house; you might want to go look there for a treasure!

As I mentioned earlier, these adventures are a lot of fun. However, a word of caution would be to make sure you have permission from private land owners and that state and national parks allow for digging and removing items.

Please do not allow this disclaimer to sway you away from this kind of adventure; with the right permission, you may just uncover a "national treasure." The government may not allow you to keep it, however, but they generally will give you credit and free tickets when the exhibit opens!

19
Bartering/Trading/Swapping Items

As the owner and founder of the website BarterOnly.com, how can I not talk about bartering, trading, and swapping items? Whether it's online or at a swap meet, trading can be a lot of fun (and profitable). You need an item; someone else has that item. But then guess what: you have something they want. Just like back in school, it's time to make a trade. Does this concept sound odd or complicated? Actually, the majority of the world is still on the bartering system. Therefore, in some areas of the world, it's a necessity; however, it can be fun and exciting because "one man's junk is another man's treasure!" Need a little guidance as to where and how to begin? Head on over to BarterOnly.com and check out some of the articles I have written there.

20
Restoration Projects

My wife already sees this one coming when I retire—starting and hopefully finishing another restoration project. Prior to writing this book, I restored a 1978 Corvette. My mother has always been amazed and has wondered how I was able to do this. It's quite simple: I took tractor mechanics in high school and know how to watch YouTube videos. Don't think that a restoration project is too complicated—with a little effort and by knowing the right people, you too can restore anything, from cars, to boats, to Coke machines, to any other antique item. There is no satisfaction like that of bringing history back to life. Find your interest, combine it with a dose of passion, and add some effort, and you have a project that will be educational and fulfilling.

21
Garage Sale-ing, Antiquing, and Storage Auctioning

Well, folks, the adventure of garage sale-ing, antiquing, and storage auctioning is quite a broad idea; however, there is a lot of overlap to assist in exploring this dynamic. Generally, the best deals on purchases can be found at garage sales. The average garage sale lists items for a fraction of the original cost. However, the actual value of these items can be realized for a profit if sold in a different circumstance. You will find bargain hunters scouring garage sales looking for items to resell. Savvy retirees can purchase quantities of these items and resell them through auctions online or live local auctions. Not everybody finds a hidden treasure that is worth thousands of dollars, but with the proper effort, you can find some treasures and resell them for profit. A lot of people make a living doing this. My suggestion is that you do it to supplement your income with some "fun" money and for the adventure of treasure hunting. (A treasure is in the eye of the beholder.)

Here are two little hints: 1) Make sure you have Internet available on your cell phone while you are shopping so that you can research the value of items as you come across them. 2) Just because someone is asking a particular price doesn't mean that's what it is valued at.

22
Starting a Scrapbook

Here's the moment you may have been talking about for your entire career: you've always wanted to scrapbook, but you have never had time. Well, time is what you have, and it's time to get cracking. Scrapbooking stores are popping up all over the nation, with groups and classes forming all the time. The groups and classes start with the most basic and progress on up to the most complete methods of scrapbooking. A word of warning—I have had to remove my wife from the scrapbooking store because she would get so involved that it was like a full-time job for her. Have fun doing this for the grandkids. Have fun doing this for your kids. Not only is scrapbooking rewarding for you, but the scrapbooks make awesome holiday gifts.

23
Raising Livestock / Breeding Small Animals

There is a joke that goes around in the horse industry, and it goes like this: "How do you make a small fortune in the horse business?" The answer is this: "Start with a large one." With scrapbooks, you probably shouldn't go in with the hopes of making a lot. However, in the case of raising livestock or breeding small animals, it's not always a losing battle. I have a few clients who train and breed dogs. Most of the time they exceed their expenses with income. My aunts turn a minor profit most of the time, but mostly they enjoy it more than they are concerned with making money.

My action plan to incorporate this in my daily life is:

_____

_____

_____

_____

_____

_____

_____

_____

_____

_____

_____

_____

_____

III

Creative Activities

As I am being creative to create this book, so must you be during retirement. Although I may be creating this book for a business purpose, I am also exercising my mind through the use of creativity. In the same respect, as you age, you must do the same. However, just as a person will exercise his or her muscles to maintain physical fitness, so must everyone when it comes to the mind.

In this section, we will explore various adventures that utilize the mind. I highly recommend that every retiree undergo at least one of the adventures in this section or one of the intellectual ones in the next in order to maintain mental fitness.

24
Starting a Blog

No formal writing experience is required to start a blog. A blog is strictly made up of your ideas and opinions. Your blog can cover any topic or subject matter of conversation. A blog can also be random in nature when it comes to ideas. What is your passion, your interest, your knowledge…today? Write an article and post it. Millions of people scour the Internet daily looking for information to read. What's that? You say you don't have any information that you can write about? Then write about someone else, their life, their adventures, their anecdotes. Have fun with it!

I will be discussing this later, however, I must mention here that you can set up advertisements on your blog page and get paid! Don't expect it to be much, but money is money. However, if you provide a lot of content and keep up with your blog on a regular basis, you will end up attracting a lot of people. In the Internet world, people equals traffic, and traffic equals money!

25
Hosting a Podcast

Maybe writing is not your forte, but speaking is. How about developing and hosting a podcast? Ever thought about interviewing the stars, but afraid of the camera? Podcasts are the latest and greatest form of media. What's that? You can't think of something to talk about? What about helping friends who own a business and asking them to write out a description of one of their processes and then recording the message and posting it on their website? What about recording an event or discussion and then uploading it onto the website? The possibilities are endless. But remember, not everybody has the time (or desire) to watch a video. There may be something out there that people are interested in listening to while working out, driving, or doing some other activity.

26
Creating How-To Videos

Unlike creating podcasts, this adventure is about creating how-to videos on YouTube. You may be sitting there a little perplexed and saying, "I don't know how to make a video on YouTube." Well, all you have to do is to go to YouTube and search "how to put a video on YouTube." Guess what you'll find? A how-to video.

The next statement you may make is, "I don't know what to talk about." Let me help you out here, as I have searched YouTube for information on how to do just about anything and everything. I, like many Americans, am too lazy to read the instructions, and so I revert to visuals to explain. Technology has allowed for masses to follow a visual presentation better than written instructions. Therefore, take anything that you know how to make or do (e.g., the best cookie in the world, a cool birdhouse, changing a car tire); explain what you are teaching the viewer to do; and then publish it on YouTube. It doesn't matter how simple or complex you get; people are going to watch your video. Always remember—your subject doesn't have to be new to the world, just a new or easier way of explaining something. The only people who don't need to watch how-to videos on YouTube are people who already know it all, and last I checked, there weren't that many people who were bona fide geniuses.

27
Making Homemade Movies

A buddy of mine got me into the next adventure. He has a website called Buckheadhunting.com. Basically he showed me how easy it is to make a movie just by using his iMac. Whether it's the classic home-movie compilation of your family vacations or the next *Blair Witch Project*, making a movie can be fun and, if you utilize YouTube properly, profitable.

Just like for how-to videos, if you are not sure about how to make a movie, go to YouTube and search "how to make a movie." Yes, it's as simple as it gets.

28
Writing a Book

I once heard that the human mind contains enough knowledge to fill a library with books. Therefore, if your mind can fill a library, why not write a book? Just as I have written this book, you too can write a book. Really, a book such as this is one of the easiest types of book to write. First, take a notebook sheet of paper. (Yes, we are doing this the "old school" way.) Then number the lines 1 through 99. Now think of your topic: ninety-nine ways to cook carrots, ninety-nine ways to get out of a speeding ticket, ninety-nine ways to landscape your backyard, and so on. If you can only think of thirty-five ideas, then call your book *Thirty-Five Ways to Skin a Cat*. This is the simple way to write a book.

If you can't seem to come up with a topic, write about your life, someone else's life, or your career, or use your memoirs. Keeping it personal will allow you to get more in depth in terms of subject matter, and I suggest you write about a field you have some expertise in. A buddy of mine has written several military books. Because of his top-secret clearance in the military, he had to convert the books to fiction. Therefore, if you can't think of anything informative to write about, then write a fictional story. I promise you that the world of readers will always find room for another book.

29
Interviewing Elders in Your Community

Prior to formal education systems, most of the world was unable to read or write. Therefore, stories were passed down verbally. The greatest way to record history is to interview elders in your community and record their memories and anecdotes. This does not have to be in a formal book form. Even just taking notes in a spiral-bound notebook would be sufficient. Just as you were interested in recording the memory or anecdote, someone else will most likely be interested in reading it. Refer back to the section on starting a blog or writing a book to find creative ways to have your recordings preserved and shared with others.

30
Learning Ceramics, Pottery, and Sculpture

As I was developing these ideas, certain influential people in my own life came to mind. One of those people is my aunt Cindy. Prior to retiring, she made beautiful pottery. My hope is that she reads this book and, now that she is retired, starts making pottery again. I urge everyone to learn a hobby. You can start by looking into how to make ceramics, pottery, or sculptures. Yes, artistic attributes are a plus, but most teachers of this craft tell me that patience is the most important attribute in creating "masterpieces." I put quotes around masterpieces, but remember, beauty is in the eye of the beholder. My aunt will talk down about her work, but I think her creations are fantastic!

31
Studying Interior Design

This next one I came up with because I think that most people desire the niceties in life but don't have the education to design or decorate. How about a study in interior design? I love my wife with all my heart, but when it comes to decorating, she doesn't have the background to catapult her creativity. Study as an apprentice under an interior decorator, take some online courses, or enroll in a college that offers the courses. You may not have a desire to become a full-time interior designer, but you may develop a simple "touch of charm" that will *wow* all your friends.

32
Designing and Making Clothing

Creativity and the skill to follow directions are the characteristics you'll need for the next adventure: designing and making clothing. Walk into a fabric store and you will see that the biggest obstacle in making clothing is learning how to follow directions that come with the patterns. Most people think that sewing is difficult; however, I remember sewing pants and a tie in high school. I can still today put a hem in my pants and sew up a hole. How did I learn this? I took a class, of course. This class happened to be given by an individual, but most sewing centers also offer sewing classes. Any specialty store that sells sewing equipment generally offers classes. The reason behind this is to spark more interest so they can sell more products.

Classes range from those designed for beginners and move on up to advanced. There are many sewing groups/clubs that meet and generally advertise meetings at sewing centers.

33
Crafting Items for Donation

So, you want to leave this world a better place than how you found it? Couple that idea with your creativity, and you have your next adventure: crafting items for donation. Churches, civic groups, and other organizations often host various fund-raising activities. Therefore items such as art projects, birdhouses, decorative items for the home, or homemade blankets would be possibilities, but your skills and imagination are what will further this adventure.

Although I don't condone the behavior, people seem to want to receive something in return when donating. The secondary benefits that carry forward from doing this adventure could include advertising of your craft through the recognition received and potential tax advantages that come with donations to eligible organizations.

34
Building a Point of Interest

Have you ever visited the world's largest ball of twine in Cawker City, Kansas, the teapot in Chester, West Virginia, or the thermometer in Baker, California? Well, they had to start somewhere! What an adventure it would be to build a point of interest. It can be something serious, funny, or informative, or whatever you want it to be. Let your mind do the work of exploring ideas.

Whether the idea is for personal usage, for a good laugh, or to see how much attention you can generate, the adventure (fun) is in the doing!

As a character said in the movie *Field of Dreams*, "If you build it, they will come." When saying "they" here, I am referring to other retirees, most of whom have not read this book and are bored out of their minds. Those who have read this book stop to log this point of interest on their Life Adventure Inventory Sheet (located in the final chapter), which they will write about in their book, blog, or video diary.

35
Inventing a New Device

For those looking for the most creative adventure, inventing a new device may be the right choice for you. Not everybody can just wake up one morning and say, "I'm going to invent something new." Have you ever thought to yourself when you saw a new invention, "Why didn't I think of that?" or "I had the same idea a few years ago"? It may be beyond your capacity, but maybe you do have the innovative nature inside of you. An invention does not have to be a physical product that you operate by hand; today in the technological age, an invention can be a new website. An invention is just a product that is new and assists in performing a task.

Here are a couple of things to remember before you get started:

1. Don't forget to document the development of your idea step by step; then at least if someone steals your idea, you have documentation (or you can turn it into a book).
2. Don't think you have to have a lot of money to invent something. If your product is worthwhile, someone will pay to build it for you.
3. If you invent a product, don't forget to patent it. In case your invention already was patented (someone already thought of it), you can modify the idea and it still may get patented.

4. Don't fall for those invention-idea companies. Most are just a scam, and very few ever get a product picked up by a manufacturer.

Now, put on your thinking cap and start designing!

36
Naming a New Star

If you ever do the research online, you will discover that "Name a Star" is the name of a novelty gift company. The fact is that the International Astrological Union (IAU) does not recognize the names from the companies that "sell" the naming of the stars. However, if you are up for a really unique and recognizable adventure, find a new star and name it. Currently there are approximately 945 million cataloged stars. Just like in Hollywood, stars are born and die all the time. Therefore, search the nighttime sky and you may just discover a new star, comet, asteroid, or alien spacecraft. But remember, if you discover it, you have to name it, and the IAU will then assign a number to it.

37
Transferring Old Videos/Pictures to Modern Media

I can say that this next adventure idea was taken from the many projects that my mother took on in the onset of her retirement. To occupy her time she would transfer old videos/pictures onto new technology. Whether it was scanning in pictures and saving them to a CD or transferring old eight-millimeter films to VHS and then to DVD, this provided her hours of unending work. But even this process is not complete for dear Mom.

Technology has now advanced to the point that she can spend more time transferring media to the hard drive on her computer or to the "cloud." Too bad the cloud was not available when she began this process. She could have skipped a step, like you can now!

More importantly what I like about this adventure is that it provides you time to reminisce about the past and relive the times when the pictures were taken.

I should put a dollar sign next to this adventure because if you were to get good and creative, you could charge all of those other people who don't have time for transferring their old videos and/or pictures to modern media. All it takes is one fire in your house and you will regret never having done this, because in today's high-tech world, once the items have been transferred to digital format, they can be uploaded and secured from ever being damaged.

38
Learning to Play an Instrument

Here's a new and creative idea: learn to play an instrument. A friend of mine recently retired, and she learned to play the piano. My wife and I talk about taking banjo lessons (it's a Southern thing); however, our busy schedule prevents us from setting aside the time to do so. Also, studies have proven that children who learn to play a musical instrument have improved math skills, and the same should apply to mental acuteness in adults. Has there ever been an instrument you've yearned to learn?

My action plan to incorporate this in my daily life is:

_____

_____

_____

_____

_____

_____

_____

_____

_____

_____

_____

_____

_____

IV

Intellectual Challenges

Ever heard the famous slogan, "The mind is a terrible thing to waste"? No matter how young or old you are, when people stop exercising their mind because they do not recognize the need, their mental and physical health begin to deteriorate. The mind must be continually challenged to stay active. Whether it is through independent creative thinking or formal intellectual enrichment, the quintessential determination of longevity is the willingness to challenge the mind to constant exercise.

This chapter challenges the mind to continually process new information. Although at first glance at the section title you may have thought that this section would be solely dedicated to learning, regular maintenance is another great aspect to include. As I have always told clients and associates, "As long as my noodle still operates, I can make a supportive living to provide for my family."

39
Learning a New Language

Learning a new language is one of my favorite adventures. There is nothing less true than the old adage, "You can't teach an old dog new tricks." It is a lie. Anybody at any age can learn a new language. As a retiree, your time is dedicated to freedom! Anybody can learn a language, at least on a conversational level, in four to six months by just practicing for one hour a day, five days a week. By the time I turn sixty, my goal is to have learned four languages. In the summer of 2014, my goal was to learn a conversational level of Spanish. My next goal is to learn French.

How do I learn these languages in a land where my native tongue predominates? If you don't practice it every day, how can you learn the language? Choose a method that works best for you; immersion, computer software, language courses at a nearby college, hire a tutor or develop a friendship with a native speaker, you are only limited by your imagination.

So, what's holding you back? Time? You've made it this far in life, so it's not intelligence. Try it; you won't fail. I promise.

40
Going (Back) to College

If Rodney Dangerfield could do it, you can, too. Go back to college or get started if you haven't gone before. Whether you already have a degree or want to pursue a new degree, gaining or extending an upper-level education will occupy a tremendous amount of your time. Going to a traditional college does not always have to be your course of action for this adventure; what about culinary school, art school, technical trade school, seminary, and so forth? The ideas are limitless. In the past, I've heard people say, "I'm too old to go back to college." I've never understood this phrase, since I am constantly reading about eighty- and ninety-year-olds graduating from college. Also, I read all the time about former executives going to seminary or culinary school to pursue a dream they've always had.

41
Reading

Outside of my father's fifty million items on my mom's honey-do list, he likes to make an escape through mental adventures. That's right; he loves to read. Reading may seem monotonous, but take control of this adventure and mix it up. Challenge yourself to do what you have never done before. If you are non-fiction person, try mixing it up and read fiction. Another idea is to choose a long series of novels and read through it. For those who are not avid readers, don't force yourself to start reading; you will bore yourself to death.

42
Auditing College Classes and Lectures

So college is too expensive or maybe too much of a commitment? Why not audit college classes? To audit a class is to take a class without the benefit of a grade. You do it for self-enrichment or academic exploration. Generally colleges and universities will allow you to sit on classes; however, it is always limited to space availability. What about if you were to sit in on lectures? Maybe a full semester is too time consuming, or maybe there is a presenter who will be speaking to a particular class or on a topic you would like to learn more about. Most colleges allow you to attend these lectures, again, based on space availability. The college or university's goal is to pique your interest and get you

to enroll in the classes; however, if it is a state-funded university, the goal is to educate the taxpayers in that state.

43
Researching Your Genealogy

I have mentioned my mother throughout this book because of the fact that she is living proof that "a rolling stone gathers no moss." One of her current tasks at hand is to research genealogy, and she has really gotten into it. Because of the ease of using Ancestry.com coupled with the program Family Tree Maker, she has been able to streamline the research process needed to create a family tree that dates further back than those created in traditional libraries. Technology has allowed a world of genealogical research to be harnessed into one area. Using this research, she has been able to submit membership requests to organizations that require proof of genealogical identity, such

as the Daughters of the American Revolution. Also, being that this information is now captured digitally, this work will not be lost like most family trees developed by previous generations.

44
Brain-Strengthening Exercises

The key to longevity is keeping the mind sharp. Once a person's mental state has deteriorated, his or her bodily functions begin to shut down. Brain-strengthening exercises, which can be found on various websites, assist in keeping the mind youthful. Just as it is important to get daily exercise for your body, your brain also requires constant exercise and activity. Websites such as Lumosity.com assist in exercising the mind. Also, the Nintendo 3DS has a game called Brain Age. In addition, Sudoku, crossword puzzles, and trivia games can also be very advantageous to exercising the brain. These are just a few examples of brain-strengthening exercises. You can explore the Internet for other great activities. At first it may seem juvenile to play a game, but researchers have proven that these exercises can effectively improve your chances of longevity and quality of life. Seriously, instead of sitting in front of the TV (which adds zero value to anyone's life), pick up one of these activities and engage yourself in this adventure in your downtime.

My action plan to incorporate this in my daily life is:

_____

_____

_____

_____

_____

_____

_____

_____

_____

_____

_____

_____

_____

V

Social and Family Events

I used to do hospital ministry, and it never failed when I walked into a terminally ill person's room. We would start a conversation, and then about ten to fifteen minutes into the conversation, people would start to give me advice based on mistakes they had made in their own life. The number-one mistake was that they didn't spend enough time with family, and number two was not spending enough time with friends. What I am stating is not a scientific fact; merely an observation. I spoke to a lot of people, and I never had someone tell me that he or she wished to have spent more time at work.

Because of logistics and distance, I did not spend a lot of time with my grandparents. However, my memories are filled with those times when I was able to enjoy their company. Allow me to pass on this advice prior to getting to the point of regret: Spend as much time now with family as possible. There are people who could use your experience and knowledge through the advice you give; go out and see them.

45
Joining Clubs and Organizations

There have been many books written and many studies conducted about humans' need for social interaction. This was the theme of the movie *Castaway*, where Tom Hanks uses a volleyball in order to attempt to achieve social interaction. To increase your level of social interaction, join a social club, fitness group, book club, professional sorority, or any other social organization. If you do not walk away from this book with anything useful, you might take a look at this idea more closely. I have stated two keys to longevity: physical and mental acuteness. The most important aspect of mental acuteness is that of social interaction. You say, "But I just want to retire and be left alone"? *Bull!* You may not need it in large doses, but you will need some interaction to survive.

In addition to the interaction aspect, clubs and groups require that you have an agenda to plan for, responsibilities to live up to, and other individuals to motivate you. Nobody can self-motivate all of the time.

46
Associating with People Younger than You

You've heard the adage "Birds of a feather flock together"; yep, it's true, but as a retiree, if you associate with people younger than you, it will drive you to be active as if you were younger. Don't just take my word for it; ask your doctor or google it. If you spend your time with younger people who maintain a healthy lifestyle, you will also inherit that healthy lifestyle. The youthful energy will also carry over to you. Still don't believe me? Go hang out with someone ten years older than you and then someone ten years younger than you and see when you are more active.

By the way, I'm not suggesting you should be a stalker and impose upon your younger friends in their private time; I'm suggesting that you should hang out with them when they are out and about. And you should still hang out with your older friends since they are the ones who have the wisdom.

47
Nannying Your Grandkids

One of my all-time favorite quotes is "Parents like their kids; they *love* their grandkids." Here's your chance to spoil the ever-living heck out of your grandkids by being a nanny to them. Sacrifice your time to be the one who spoils those kids, and then send them home to Mom and Dad. Here's where you get to combine adventures: you are associating with people younger than you, and you are definitely going to get your exercise.

And don't forget, by being a nanny to the grandkids, you are saving Mom and Dad a lot of money on daycare. Ask for a little financial consideration for your time and efforts.

48
Visiting Friends and Family

Every day when I drive home from work, I see a billboard that says, "Talk to a stranger, call your family." Better yet, you are retired, so pack up the Cadillac and go visit friends and family. I'm not asking for you to seek out every family member up and down your family tree, but I am suggesting that you connect with family members who have been "ignored" due to the fact of logistics.

49
Attending a Marriage Retreat

For those who are married, it's time now to fall in love all over again. Whether you are renewing your wedding vows or just want to attend a marriage retreat and rejuvenate your marriage, now is the time to do it. For thirty-plus years, you have dedicated your waking days to your profession, but now those waking days are filled with being at home with your spouse. Uh, yes, it's just the two of you day in, day out, till death do you part. You might be saying, "Oh my, we haven't had this much alone time together since we first started dating!" Now is a great time to learn how to live together every day. Make an annual pilgrimage to a marriage conference; you get to travel, you get to be with your mate, and you get to have fun. But don't forget: pick a location that you have never been to before or somewhere the both of you will enjoy seeing together after the conference.

50
Organizing a Family Reunion

So, you're a glutton for punishment? Well here's an adventure for you, and boy is it an adventure. How about organizing a family reunion? Now, I didn't exactly name this book *99 Fantastic Ideas!* Here are a couple of tips to save you some sanity:

1. You will never please everybody. With this in mind...
   a. Send out an e-mail to family members to ask everyone's opinion about dates and locations. But keep things simple and only give three of each to choose from.
   b. Once you receive the replies, select the most popular choices for dates and locations and the ones that best accommodate you, the organizer.
2. Do not pay for anybody's portion in expectation that they will pay you back.
3. Do not put down a monetary deposit to rent a location for the event by yourself. Have family members pay their own deposits.

4. If you are going to use a credit card to hold your portion of the venue, use a credit card that will expire prior to the event. Don't get stuck with the bill because Uncle Albert died two days before the reunion and everyone is going to his funeral instead.
5. Make sure there is some sort of "escape clause" in the contract so that you are not left holding the bill.
6. Learn fast how to delegate tasks.

Other than those simple tips, have fun!

51
Creating a Family Cookbook

Creating a family cookbook can be a very delicious adventure. It can also be an opportunity to make some money. The greatest thing about food is that there will never be too many recipes. There are always dozens of new cookbooks being published and hitting the shelves, so why shouldn't the next one be yours? Gather up family recipes, retype them in digital formats, and then compile them into one book, and then sell your book. What—you don't think it's that easy? Well, it is. In this day and age, self-publishing is the route to go. You can create this cookbook and publish it through Amazon or Apple, just to name a few. These days, you don't need to publish a hard-copy book; putting your recipes on a website is enough and may reach more people than a traditional book. I have a friend who has the website Kitchenbelleicious.com, which is a fantastic source for ideas on cooking. Why can't you similarly create a family cookbook website and blog?

By the way, if you need to check the quality of the recipes in your family's cookbook, prepare them and then give me a call. I would be more than happy to sample food and give you an honest opinion!

52
Starting a Family Tradition/Legacy

It all starts somewhere with the work of someone, so why can't you be the one who starts a family tradition/legacy? The ideas are limitless, but the traditions that last the longest are those that every family member can take ownership of. This can be as simple as a pair of gold cufflinks passed down for generations or something more intriguing, like the family tree you have worked on. It can even be an annual trip to a state park. My favorite is establishing a scholarship or endowment fund in the family's name. Most nonprofit organizations will have some form of a policy to allow for named grants or scholarships. Generally there are rules as to minimums, but how cool would it be to know that no matter what happens out there in the world, you may be gone but your legacy will affect the lives of others whom you have never met?

Kyle A Sadler, AIF, CRC

My action plan to incorporate this in my daily life is:

_____

_____

_____

_____

_____

_____

_____

_____

_____

_____

_____

_____

VI

Travel Adventures

Even though we're still talking about adventures for retirees, we have to expand the preconceived notions that most retirees envision upon their retirement. Although you may connect traveling to getting in a boat, airplane, or car and heading to your destination for a week or two, this section will explore true adventures and hopefully entice you to think outside the norm when it comes to traveling.

53
Going on a Vacation

The first idea is the simplest yet the most difficult to do during retirement: going on a vacation. It's obvious that once a person retires, his or her first instinct is to travel to a vacation destination. So go do it.

Now that you have made the mistake of traveling to that place advertised on the Internet that turned out to be a waste of time and vacation money, let's talk about real vacationing. Why do I say this? Because during my life I have heard over and over again, "I need a vacation from my vacation." This mistake is made because 98 percent of vacationers do not know how to vacation. I can't tell you exactly where to go, but I sure can tell you how to determine the right destination:

1. Determine what type of activity is relaxing to you.
2. Determine the cost of that activity.
3. Practice the activity you'll be doing one weekend at your house...for the entire weekend. The reason I say this is because people will often tell you to just relax and sleep on your vacation. Seriously, can you spend all weekend in your house sleeping and doing nothing? You say, "But it's different when I'm on vacation"? No, it's not.
4. Imagine where you find true blissful happiness.

5. Imagine the location.
6. Imagine your attire, the people who will be with you, the air temperature, the noise, the smells.
7. Don't look for vacation destinations on the Internet; no site in the world advertises what you truly want on your vacation. You have to search the Internet to discover the story of where someone has been that is similar to the experience and adventure you truly desire.

I am no different from the next person—I love Groupon and LivingSocial; however, I promise that nobody advertises the vacation of your dreams on those websites. It's time to be creative; it's time to discover the true meaning of the relaxation of retirement.

By the way, the best and most memorable vacations don't cost a lot of money. Think back to the most fun you have ever had in your life—I bet there wasn't a huge price tag associated with it.

54
Hiking in an Exotic Place

For a more active adventure, hiking on a glacier or seeing the northern lights can be wonderful experiences. Some of the ideas that I mention in this book come from my personal bucket list. Therefore, I toss them out to help retirees think of activities they can do themselves. There are many ways to reach these destinations: taking Carnival Cruise Lines via Vancouver to Alaska or taking a helicopter ride out of Anchorage are just a few options.

55
Visiting the Seven Wonders of the World
For anyone who has ever done research, there are many types of wonders in this world. Why not visit the Seven Wonders of the World? The reason I stated that there are many types of wonders is because in the classification, there are seven natural wonders, seven man-made wonders, and various others. Try doing a few Google searches and think about the destinations you find as travel choices.

56
Visiting the Country of Your Ancestral Origin
Visiting the country of your ancestral origin is my wife's and my next adventure. How cool it will be to walk on the same grounds on which my ancestors once worked, played, and congregated. Thanks to my mother's genealogical research, I can now look up any location to which my former relatives traveled and visit their native land. You never know; you may even meet a distant cousin while traveling on this adventure.

57
Spending a Year Overseas
Throughout the book *The 4-Hour Work Week*, Timothy Ferriss discusses miniretirements. In the spirit of miniretirements, spend a year overseas. You may be contemplating retiring from what you are currently doing for income, but are you also planning on retiring from life? You are probably reading this book to come up with ideas to fill your time throughout retirement. As I stated earlier in the book, the secret to

longevity is staying active. My simple prescription—retire from what you are doing. Live abroad in an area where US products and services have a particularly high value and are not found often (in the majority of the world, you can live on one-third to one-half of what you are currently spending). Rent a house for a year and enjoy learning a new culture (and the native tongue).

58
Geocaching

Scavenger hunts have gone high tech. Today, with the assistance of GPS systems, geocaching is the new way of doing scavenger hunts. If you're thinking, "This is a game for kids," just google geocaching and read up on it; then go out and try it. I promise you that it's a blast.

59
Going to Adult Summer Camps

For those who are new to retirement, summer camp isn't just for kids anymore. Just like the ones you went to back in the day, now there are summer camps for adults. You can also "pick your poison": do you want to rough it out or stay in air-conditioned camp houses? The experience is fantastic, and most of the camps are very affordable. Yes, like youth camp, you will have crafts to do and outdoor activities such as canoeing, and a lot of times there are dances. For singles or couples, these camps are held worldwide. Just do a Google search for "adult summer camps" and discover the possibilities.

60
Taking River, Ocean, and Lake Cruises

A favorite bucket-list item of my wife's and mine is to do a river cruise through Amsterdam, Holland, and Northern Europe.

Ocean and lake cruises are another popular way to see the world. Although lake and river cruises are not popular in the United States, in Europe they are very popular. One such cruise line is Viking Cruises. The company has complete all-inclusive packages containing not only food, transfers, and accommodations, but also airfare. Remember to explore your options, because there is more to the world than just your hometown.

61
Visiting State and National Parks

As I mentioned in other sections, some of the best views and sights can be seen when you visit state and national parks. Whether you are there for a short day trip or overnight, these parks offer a wide assortment of amenities and activities. Just by visiting a state or national park, you will conquer multiple adventures listed in this book. The really great news is that a lot of the parks offer free or extremely discounted admission for senior adults. So, load up the car with the grandkids and have an enjoyable day at the park.

My action plan to incorporate this in my daily life is:

_____

_____

_____

_____

_____

_____

_____

_____

_____

_____

_____

_____

VII

Spiritual Journeys

One of two ideas probably popped into your mind when you read the title of this chapter: church or mediation. Yep, both answers are correct; however, let's dive a little deeper into this topic. The reason is the same as one discussed previously: spiritual journeys alter preconceived notions about what can constitute an adventure. In this section, we will explore ideas that a common person might not assume would fall under this topic.

62
Meditation

Peace, love, and harmony are the keys to mental health. These are achieved by people who practice meditation. Unfortunately, meditation is taken out of context a lot of times because of a lack of understanding. A lot of people think that the only form of meditation is the classic chanting of "om" or some other mantra. However, meditation is the clearing of the mind to become calm and silent. As a Christian, I utilize mediation in order to do my biblical studies and prayers. Trust me, meditation is not easy, and to clear the mind takes a lot of practice. Once you have achieved a calm and silent mind, controlled thoughts and, in my case, prayers, become easier.

63
Making a Pilgrimage

Pack your bags (or just come as you are) and become a pilgrim. Commit yourself to visit a site or sites that are meaningful to your spiritual life. Going on a pilgrimage as an act of faith has been an integral part of religious life for centuries and now you have the time to do it. Because of the vast number of possibilities, you would want to search the Internet for locations pertinent to your faith. Whether it's to the Holy Land, a monastery, or the site of an ancient temple, you have to remember that a pilgrimage is about the journey and not the distance or cost.

64
Participating in Mission Work
(Domestic or International)

This next adventure is my wife's and my passion: mission work (domestic or international)! Although we have traveled on international missions, the main mission work we've done has been helping those in our community. Mission work can be as simple as washing dishes at a soup kitchen and can get as involved as sharing the gospel in China. The whole purpose of this type of work is to further God's kingdom. Therefore, discover your purpose and utilize any and all talents that you

may have to serve others. And before you start making excuses as to why you can't serve in one capacity or another, please note that I have been on mission trips with seventy-five-year-olds, unemployed individuals who didn't have a dime to their name, and agnostics. Just like them, you can do it! Life is about sharing and giving what you have, and once you do these things, you will be forever rewarded.

As for my wife and me, our goal at retirement is to do international mission work for unreached populations. Actually, if you bought this book, 100 percent of the money we receive from your purchase will go toward mission work. If you would like to find some ways you can serve in missionary work, please contact me or your pastor. We would be delighted to share some ideas with you.

65
Caring for the Homebound or Elderly

The next adventure could be characterized as a mission project, although it certainly doesn't have to be approached in that manner. Spend time caring for the homebound or in nursing homes. You may be thinking it's awkward to deal with such people, but I hate to say it, you may be in their position in the next twenty to thirty years yourself. Wouldn't you want someone to come and visit you? Your answer may be, "I wouldn't want a stranger coming to see me. I wouldn't know what to talk about." But those who are homebound or in a nursing home don't care if they have a scripted Q&A time; all they care about is that someone is making them feel like they are the most important person in the world. Your presence (and a plate of cookies wouldn't hurt either) is all they are looking for. They need you in order to stay alive.

My action plan to incorporate this in my daily life is:

_____

_____

_____

_____

_____

_____

_____

_____

_____

_____

_____

_____

_____

VIII

Volunteer Activities

This chapter is probably the most important one in this book. Whether it was the fact that my roots when growing up were deeply embedded in 4-H or that my parents taught me to give back to the community more than I take away, volunteering is the quintessential element of advancement of society. Humanity cannot function on proprietary organizations alone. It must rely on individuals saying, "I want to make a difference and leave this world better than how I found it." Volunteer opportunities can be found in more areas than just your local soup kitchen (although that is very important and highly recommended).

66
Learning a New Trade or Skill

My dad once said that when he retired he wanted to work in a cabinetry shop. Well, he had no actual experience building cabinets, so why would they hire him? His solution was that he would volunteer to learn a new trade or skill. If my father were to go to the owner of a cabinet shop and say, "I want to sweep the shop, help with deliveries, and be that third hand you need around the shop, and it will cost you nothing. Would you teach me to build cabinets?" After the business owner took a second to catch his or her breath, the owner more than likely would say yes. As my mom and dad used to tell me, "It never hurts to ask!"

67
Volunteering at a Church or Nonprofit

When the word "volunteer" is mentioned, the first place anyone would think of to do it is at a church or nonprofit. Therefore, this is probably the simplest adventure to write about. Churches and nonprofits cannot operate with prudent interest toward the mission of the organization without the assistance of volunteers. My belief is that everyone should volunteer for a cause at least one day a month. I urge you to find a cause that you are passionate about and volunteer as many days a month as you can. If you need help locating an organization, feel free to contact me via my website AfterURetire.com. I will get you in touch with one of several organizations I work closely with.

68
Volunteering to be a Fund-Raiser

What is a fund-raiser without volunteers? Of course it's a no-brainer that you can volunteer to be a fund-raiser, because it would be a job if you were employed to be a fund-raiser. You're retired—I don't want you to have a job. The number-one fund-raiser that comes to my mind for retirees is the March of Dimes. There are hundreds upon thousands of nonprofit organizations that need assistance fulfilling their missions, so determine where your passion lies and get to work. Remember that in addition to your traditional nonprofits, schools, churches, and hospitals also all require fund-raising.

I highly encourage you to research a nonprofit prior to engaging with it. A lot of nonprofits claim to be charitable organizations; however, as is widely discoverable on the Internet, there is more and more data supporting that some of them are fronts for very-high executive compensation and benefits. I encourage you to visit websites like Guidestar.com and Charitywatch.com to investigate the nonprofit before you choose to work for it.

69
Coaching a Team

Do you have a passion for sports? OK, let me rephrase that: Do you have a passion for children? If you do, why not coach a team? You don't have to be an expert when it comes to a sport. Heck, my wife is the furthest from knowing anything about sports, and she ended up coaching a soccer team. Most sports leagues for young children have everything laid out for how things work and provide training for coaches. Kids don't require expert coaches; they just require you to be present. I have served in many volunteer roles in my life, and a child has never come back to me five years down the road to tell me how great it was that I taught them to win; however, I have had kids grow up and tell me how great it was to know that every week, I was there for them.

70
Grant Writing

Grant writing for organizations is often done as a voluntary effort; however, a lot of organizations pay individuals to successfully write grants. If you have the ability and passion to scour through a lot of paperwork and can write an intriguing and complex proposal, there are hundreds and thousands of organizations looking for someone like you. Remember that the majority of the time with grants, the grantor will host a grant workshop to assist applicants in writing these proposals. Therefore, don't forget to account for that time when exploring this option.

71
Assisting a Professor at a College

OK, I can admit on this one that not everyone will be qualified to work on a scholarly project at a college. However, don't think that you have to be a PhD in order to work on a project. A lot of times, professors just need volunteers to be the third hand for them. (Just be careful that they're not just looking for "guinea pigs"!) Not to say that you couldn't champion a scholarly project yourself, but remember, you're retired, so take it easy. The easiest way to get involved in one of these projects is to simply call your local college and speak with the department chairs to inquire if there are any projects that you can assist with. Normally, they will issue a summary packet and requirements for volunteers. Check it out—it could be one of those things that you may find a knack for or, better yet, you might find the cure for cancer!

72
Volunteering at a Library

At the beginning of this book, I mentioned coupling ideas for additional enjoyment of the adventures. Volunteering at a library can be coupled with the idea of reading. Most library systems are receiving less and less funding due to the availability of information on the Internet for research purposes. However, libraries are also important venues for children to experience the joys of reading books. A computer will never replace the creativity and the worlds of imagination that a book can provide a child. Make it a quest to save the libraries from extinction!

73
Working at an Animal Shelter

As I have told my children over and over again in regard to our fifty million pets, "Those cages don't clean themselves!" Well, it's true; they don't. How about volunteering to work at an animal shelter? As I stated earlier, most nonprofits operate on a limited budget; therefore, any assistance, whether it's manual labor, clerical, or even event planning, is always greatly appreciated. And how rewarding of a job is getting to work with puppies and kittens!

74
Teaching English (or Another Language) Abroad

This next "volunteer" adventure, which will be my future muse, is to teach English (or another language) abroad. I call this my muse and put quotation marks around the word "volunteer"

because of the fact that as an instructor abroad, there are schools, companies, and individuals willing to pay big money to have you teach English. However, my goal is to go overseas and get services and skills in return for teaching English. Before you think that you have to have proper English skills to teach, guess again—there is always a set of guidelines available that provides a step-by-step guide on how to teach properly.

I do plan on volunteering my time upon retirement to teaching English abroad; I just didn't want to give everyone the idea that teaching English is strictly for volunteers. By all means, you should try to earn as much as you can for teaching abroad!

75
Teaching ESL at a Church or Community Center

As I sit here tonight writing this suggestion, my wife is teaching English as a second language (ESL) at a church. An adventure like this is usually a service project for the community, so please don't expect compensation to come. Immigrants come to this country for opportunity. I have traveled with mission teams and have seen the little opportunity that people have in their countries, and I've realized how blessed we are in the United States. There is little doubt as to why people want to come to our country. Teaching ESL allows them the vehicle they need to succeed in the United States. Besides, our families were all immigrants once.

Here's just a little side note: One of the ladies who takes my wife's class comes over and cleans our house. Most of the time Maria won't accept money since my wife gives her English lessons outside of the class. Because we are a giving family and Maria won't accept money, we just give her a very nice Christmas present.

76
Mentoring/Tutoring

Currently I volunteer as a mentor at a local school, and I am joined by dozens of other mentors who are retired. We also have an after-school tutoring program for the kids at our church. Getting involved in a mentoring/tutoring program is not only beneficial to the child but also selfless and extremely rewarding for you. For most of us, our desire in life is to leave this world a better place than the way we found it. What better way to change the world for the better than one child at a time? This is nothing earth shattering, but it's one of the most rewarding activities you can possibly take part in.

77
Becoming an Activist

It starts with passion, then it becomes a platform, and before you know it you have become an activist. There are those in the world who need a voice but have nobody to speak for them. There are also those who just wander with no direction or leader. That is, until someone stands up with a passion and says, "We need to make a difference; we need to change to progress!" There is no formal training. The only requirement is someone who has a passion for a cause, someone who is a leader, someone who wants to make a difference, and someone who can write a speech and present it. Today's your day to make a difference for our tomorrow...you never know, you may just end up as president of the United States.

78
Becoming a Tour Guide

The next adventure comes from my uncle Ed: becoming a tour guide for your favorite place. I never thought of this until we were on vacation visiting him while he was doing his volunteer work. He loves trains so much that he became a volunteer tour guide at the train museum. That's right—find your favorite place, go to management, and share your passion. Then tell them that you would like to volunteer as a tour guide. There are several perks to this: (a) your admission should always be free, (b) you will learn more during your volunteer time than you would have ever imagined, and (c) you will discover more people who share your same passion (people usually only visit places that interest them). Think the Smithsonian's Air and Space Museum or the San Diego Zoo is cool? Go ask if you can volunteer as a tour guide and see what happens (they may end up paying you).

79
Cleaning the Environment

Cleaning the environment can be accomplished in many ways. Whether you are recycling or picking up trash along the side of the road, our environment needs it. Because of the lackadaisical effort of a lot of people, trying to keep the environment clean is a full-time job. Just driving down the road, you will see cars that aren't maintained properly and are smoking, people throwing trash on the ground, and toxic waste being disposed of improperly. A person's lack of concern can be an opportunity for you to take a step forward and pick up after them.

So start off by taking some time when you go for a walk and take a little bag with you once or twice a week. While on your walk, pick up trash along the way and carry it home. There—you just got your exercise and made a difference!

80
Planting Trees

Along with cleaning the environment, when you plant trees in community areas, not only does it reduce pollutants, it beautifies the area. A lot of cities and communities have budgets for beautification projects; what they lack are people to do the job. Speak to your local city council representatives, and they might be able to provide the samplings. Also, a lot of local arboretums, civics clubs, or nurseries will provide you with the trees.

81
Delivering Flowers in Hospitals/Skilled-Care Facilities

Who doesn't like to get flowers? When I am in trouble with my wife (which is often), or when I just want to show her I love her, or if I want to give her a pick-me-up when she is not feeling well, I know the surefire way to encourage a smile is with flowers. The elderly and ill also need that crucial smile, and you can provide it by delivering flowers to skilled-care facilities/hospitals. The health and recovery of this select group of individuals are dependent on them having a support network. Just

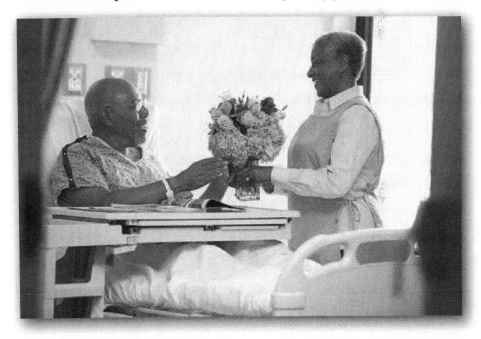

by delivering flowers, you are expressing that someone cares. Although it would be nice, I am not advocating an elaborate bouquet of flowers. If you are on a strict budget, a single flower from a stranger will bring a smile. Heck, if you decide that you want to pursue gardening through retirement as a hobby, fresh-picked flowers are always nice! (Just make sure there are no bugs in them.)

82
Being a Candy Striper at a Hospital

For the next adventure, I used a term known as a nickname when someone is volunteering at a hospital. The term "candy striper," which some of us can date back to the days of volunteers walking up and down the halls and being goodwill ambassadors to all in the hospital in red-and-white-striped uniforms. The traditional uniforms may be next to nonexistent today, but the candy striper tradition still lives on. The requirements for candy stripers vary from hospital to hospital and are also based on the talents and abilities of the individual. Volunteers may be asked to work the reception desk or gift shops, handle administrative duties such as filing and mail delivery, or deal with patient inter-action. No matter what the duty is, I always find that these men and women have the greatest hearts of anyone who visits the hospital as a patient or even of those who work there.

83
Working with the Even More Elderly

Here are two separate adventures dealing with one select group: running errands for the elderly or becoming a handyman for this group. Examples of this can be divided into three catego-ries: physical labor required, physical labor not required, and one that doesn't fit into either.

"Physical labor required" would include general home maintenance such as climbing ladders to change a lightbulb or cleaning calcium deposits out of the screens on faucets. Even more advanced skills could be utilized, such as replacing siding on a house. Physical chores for the even more elderly can build as time progresses.

Teaching others how to use a smart phone could be considered a nonphysical labor. We take for granted the level of understanding that we may possess when it comes to current technology. However, I have a client, Paula, who teaches this class, and there is always a huge turnout just to learn how to open an app on a smart phone. Even though I still haven't been able to figure it out, if you know how to program a television remote, you are in high demand.

This is the one that I couldn't classify in either of the other categories, but it is a volunteer service that cannot go unrecognized. My father was telling me of a man named Carl, who is eighty-one years old. Since he retired, he has driven a van full of veterans to the nearest veterans' affairs hospital an hour and a half away from home on a weekly to bimonthly basis. (And then he takes his wife out dancing on Saturday nights!)

As a recent retiree, you are by no means close to being incapable of filling either of these roles. And, by performing these simple acts of kindness, you are encouraging the younger generations to follow your adventurous path. Think of this as leading by example. When the time comes, this will hopefully encourage someone else to do the same and fill the void by volunteering to assist you when you become less capable.

Oh, by the way, many times you will be compensated for your efforts. If you don't feel comfortable accepting the money, then turn around and donate it to Meals on Wheels or some other elder-care nonprofit.

84

Cooking and Delivering Meals to the Homeless/Elderly

If you haven't been able to tell by now, I am a huge advocate for volunteer work. My personal belief is that you should give back to the community at least two times greater than what you take from the community. An excellent way to give back is to deliver, or to cook and deliver, meals to the homeless/elderly through Meals on Wheels or another organization. Whether it's the indigent or just people who are incapable of making meals at the current time, here's an opportunity. At our local church, when a member is ill, has had a death in the family, has been laid off, or has recently had a baby, we step up to assist in providing meals.

Just remember, there is no such thing as an age gap when it comes to a great home-cooked meal (well, at least not for me).

The smiles and happiness you will bring by sharing a meal is worth more than money itself. Don't know how to cook? Then team up with another retiree and let him or her cook and you deliver. But remember, you don't have to cook an extravagant meal, just something to nourish the person's body and relieve the stress or inability to make meals.

85
Joining a Theater Group

Would you like to stay busy for a brief period of time and then have some time in between adventures? Join a theater group and you will have just that. Usually a performance will require four to six weeks of your schedule for practicing lines and attending rehearsals. How fun it is to be on stage and share your play with the community!

Most community theaters are made up of volunteers; however, there are also several theatrical troupes or groups that provide some type of compensation. Just remember, you don't hear of millions of dollars being made as an actor or actress unless they star in a major motion picture. Therefore, don't get your hopes up that it will be worth the tank of fuel you put in (which nowadays is making it really expensive to drive).

86
Donating Your Clothes to a Local Theater

After my parents retired, they went on a spree of purging stuff in their house. My mother finally figured out that there was no need to keep my sister's and my old Halloween costumes. (I promise that they don't fit anymore.) My dad, on the other hand, discovered that, although they briefly came back in style, he was not going to be wearing those polyester bell-bottoms from the seventies. What they did discover because of my mother's involvement with the local theaters was that those bell-bottoms and old Halloween costumes were needed for costumes.

I suggest that everyone clean out their closets and donate the clothes to their local civic theater. They are always trying to raise money, but for what purpose? To afford costumes and sets. Therefore, by donating you are reducing the strain of raising funds for a production. (And if you are good with a hammer and nails or a paintbrush, they can use that help also.)

87
Working at Election Polls

At one time, I was a precinct chairman, and naturally I discovered that my best workers were retirees. I have often been quoted as saying that the most powerful lobbyists in the nation are the "blue hairs" (retired women), and I do say this with respect, tongue in cheek. The reason for this statement is that retirees possess the one commodity that we would all love to have: time. By signing up to work as an election worker, not only are you going to get paid (usually around seventy-five dollars for the day) but you are serving the cornerstone of our nation. This is not a difficult task—most of the time you are just sitting there looking at voter registration cards and verifying that the person is at the right polling location. So give this one a try—do it for your country, or at least do it for the easy money!

I understand, after rereading this adventure, you might think it's miscategorized since this is the volunteer section; it's not. Here's where the volunteer aspect comes in: most if not all jurisdictions allow you to choose whether to have your compensation donated to a charity instead of going to you. You would have probably blown the money that you would have received anyway. When someone works a one-day-a-year job, that person usually doesn't put the money into their budget—it becomes "fun money." Why not donate it to a worthy organization that could maximize the financial benefit of your easy one-day-a-year job?

88
Working on a Political Campaign

We've all heard the admonition "You can't complain if you don't vote." You can do your part to help ensure that your candidate of choice is elected to office by volunteering to work on a political campaign. Grassroots efforts are the quintessential aspect of every campaign. Constituents don't elect phone calls, posters, or billboards; they elect people. A knock on someone's door to discuss why your candidate is the right person for the job is what will influence the vote. And the yard sign or poster that you provide to that person will just be a reminder of your conversation and a way to influence the rest of the community. Democracy continues to flourish because of the grassroots efforts of volunteers.

89
Organizing a Community Festival

Age will never be a factor, because deep down we all have a little child at heart (some more than others), and what child doesn't like a good festival? Festivals don't plan themselves or become a success without someone at the helm. Someone needs to be in charge of organizing community festivals, and why not make that person you? It doesn't matter if it's an arts and crafts fair or a swap meet; heck, it can even be the local corn-and-rye festival. If you are planning a new festival, again the quote "If you build it, they will come" stands true. In its first year of existence, the festival may not attract thousands of people, but over time well-organized festivals will attract steady and increasing streams of attendees. On the other hand, if you are taking over the organization of an existing festival, keep up the awesome job that has already been done, because everyone loves a festival!

90
Volunteering at a Homeless Shelter and/or Soup Kitchen

So you claim to not be a good cook, but you want to help? A great location to lend a helping hand is at a homeless shelter and/or soup kitchen. In most cases, these facilities are run by volunteers. Funding for the building, supplies, food, and so on is generated solely from grants or fund-raising activities. Therefore, most of these organizations have limited paid staffing. I could quote several biblical verses; however, just to give a concise moral standard, we must care for those who cannot provide care for themselves.

My action plan to incorporate this in my daily life is:

_____

_____

_____

_____

_____

_____

_____

_____

_____

_____

_____

_____

_____

IX

Paid Work

Although this next section is dedicated to employment income, close to 50 percent of the ideas I have already mentioned can be incorporated into money-making ideas as well (as noted at the end of this book). Although some may not be associated with lifestyle-sustaining income, others may actually develop into an opportunity at a "second career." However, here are some additional ideas that are strictly associated with income-generating activities.

91
Signing Up for Federal Jury Duty

I had a client do this next one, and I thought he was absolutely insane for doing it. However, after he explained it, it made sense (I still think Noe's insane, but that's for other reasons—I still love him). What he did was to sign up for federal jury duty. "What?" you ask. Yes, you can sign up and serve on a federal jury. You report for six months and listen to cases and indictments. The kicker is you get paid to do it (approximately forty dollars a day). When my client was telling me about this, he said that it kept him out of the house for six months, which prevented him from getting bored and spending money. But most of all, he talked about how interesting it was to hear the different cases and see due process at work. While most of America dreads getting their local summons for jury duty, go to a federal courtroom and inquire about serving on a federal jury.

92
Substitute Teaching

If you are looking for employment after retirement with decent pay and no strings attached, consider substitute teaching at a school. I should make you aware that depending on the students you are assigned to, it may turn into quite the adventure. But most of all, you will have semi-laid-back days where the full-time teacher leaves assignments and instructions for the students; your responsibility would just be to make sure the school is not set afire in your classroom. One other minor

warning—substitute teachers normally receive the work request at 5:00 a.m. If this is acceptable to you, please, by all means do it. I will add that your willpower is stronger than mine.

93
Handing Out Free Samples at Stores

I've already mentioned what a couple of my favorite adventures would be when I retire, but handing out free samples at stores is my favorite for everybody else. I'm not talking about free soap or cologne samples; I'm talking about food. I love going to the grocery store and locating the sweet retirees who offer me delightful and tasty treats. Those people bring happiness to my life. After my wife drags me to the store, they make my shopping experience more tolerable by allowing me to experience food nirvana. Anyway, that's just my preference, but you can hand out free soap or cologne samples if that makes you happy.

94
Starting a Business

Now that you're retired, how about a new challenge: Why not start a business? Whether it's a restaurant or a novelty store, your possibilities are endless. Our former lawn guy was a licensed physical therapist at one time. After retirement, he mowed our yard for the exercise. That guy gets it! He must have met my grandmother, and her advice is worth repeating once again, "Find something you love to do and do it for the rest of your life!" Stop by your local state-funded college and speak to someone with the Small Business Association (SBA). These individuals are experts on assisting companies, from the well-established to the start-up. The advice may be free, but the information is priceless.

As I mentioned earlier in the book, the book *The 4-Hour Work Week* by Tim Ferriss may provide you with guidance on developing the line of business you should start. Another great book is *48 Days to the Work You Love* by Dan Miller. Once you have read these books, pass them on to your children, friends, and so on.

95
Selling Arts and Crafts

I wrote earlier about making arts and crafts; well, don't forget about the possibility of selling arts and crafts—that is, those items that you have made too many of for yourself and are probably giving out for gifts. You can sell them on the Internet or at trade shows. A good website for selling all sorts of arts and crafts is Etsy.com, which I highly recommend for this type of adventure. Also, if you knit, sew, or produce any other type of craft that you wish to sell online, that too is the primary purpose of Etsy.com.

Trade shows are another venue at which to sell your arts and crafts. Whether it's the big Canton Trade Days or your local arts and crafts fair, money is to be made for your hobbies of interest. Think that no one will be interested in your products? Just list them on eBay and Etsy.com to see if anybody buys before putting out your full line. If they do, most likely you have a market for your craft. However, eBay is not my preferred venue of choice for selling your arts and crafts because I find that not many people search for these types of items, so you would suggest focusing on Etsy.com or similar websites. (Craigslist would also not be recommended.)

96
Being an Extra in a Movie

My mother's passion has always been acting. Because of this passion, she was able to be an extra in a movie. She wasn't just in one movie but in multiple movies and TV shows. Being an extra will not make you rich; in fact, not all roles actually pay. However, the opportunity to grace the silver screen can far surpass the meaningless pay that you receive. In my mom's case, what she received went directly into the gas tank. Mom may not live forever, but I can turn on a movie and see my mother long after she is gone.

97
Becoming a Consultant in Your Former Industry

It's frightening to witness the amount of people I speak to on a daily basis who don't have a plan before they retire. For some reason, they automatically think at a certain point, "I'm sixty, so I must retire," but a staggeringly large number of them really

aren't ready to retire. They just feel this obligation because of their age or their years in the industry. If you are one of those people who enjoys their industry but just doesn't want to work a forty-hour-plus work week, become a consultant in your former industry. The greatest aspect of being a consultant is that you become the driver: controlling your hours, controlling your travel, controlling your stress. Over the years you have accumulated a wealth of knowledge; now it's time to maximize that intellectual property and receive compensation for offering what that slick college graduate trying to break into the industry doesn't have—experience.

98
Being a Mystery Shopper or Product Sampler

Back in the late nineties, being a mystery shopper or product sampler (one whom a company hires to check on a store's service quality, price comparison, or consumer opinion) was all the rage. Well, it's back, but the sources of service and product quality control have become separated into traditional retail outlets and Internet blogs. There are not as many retail stores as there were back then due to the decline in physical shopping; however, big-box retailers are slowly discovering that people are beginning to gravitate back to the outlets because they miss the customer service that the Internet cannot provide. Retail stores have begun to have a resurgence of mystery shoppers. Although the Internet provides leaner costs, consumers are finding that price doesn't always matter. Therefore, these retailers are looking for ways to improve the customer experience. Mystery shopping is not limited to retailers; watchdog groups and market research companies also utilize them. But use caution when applying for this position: there are a lot of scammers advertising out there.

Then there are the bloggers: product samplers now receive samples of products and then blog about them on their own website. If you are interested, you will need to establish a blogging website. However, the dynamics have changed: you won't get to sample big-name products until the number of visitors to your website achieves a competitive level. Therefore, to start out, you may have to sample the latest flavored bag of chips until you are well established.

99
Starting a New Career

So you're retired...now what? Start a new career! We've all heard that fifty is the new thirty, and sixty is the new forty. What kind of job have you always wanted to take but never had the guts to try? Or what kind of career have you always had passion for but have not wanted to pursue because you felt trapped in your current career? Well, now's your chance. You're retired, you have retirement income to support you—what do you have to lose? My mom always loved acting, but she couldn't support our family with an acting career, so immediately upon retirement, she followed that passion. Well, it's not so much of a career because of the lack of financial compensation, but thanks to her pension, she is now able to pursue a career that she would have loved to have been involved in at the onset of her work life. I have also had many other clients who have pursued other career directions that are almost a 180-degree transformation from their previous careers. You're not getting any younger, so get to work!

My action plan to incorporate this in my daily life is:

_____

_____

_____

_____

_____

_____

_____

_____

_____

_____

_____

_____

Conclusion

The following is what I call the Life Adventure Inventory Sheet, and it is comprised of the list of the adventures previously discussed. After you review the chapters and decide what interests you, keep it handy and check off each of the activities you engage in. You may be thinking that this is just a checklist; no, checklists are for chores! View this as a scorecard, and you will start to see how much you are accomplishing...and how many things are yet to be done.

As I close this book, I remember the words of my grandma: "Find something you love to do, and do it for the rest of your life."

	To Do	Doing	Done	Potential Income?
Move to the country				
Move to the city				
Remodel house				X
Move to a different city once a year				
Conquer a fear				

	To Do	Doing	Done	Potential Income?
Set a world record				
Mine for gems				X
Hunt for fossils and artifacts				X
Exercise daily				
Hike every nature trail within a two-hour radius				
Garden				X
Focus on your current hobby				X
Start a new hobby				X
Knit, crochet, quilt, needlepoint				X
Practice woodworking				X
Play golf				
Beach comb in all coastal states				X
Participate in metal detecting				X
Barter, trade, and swap items				X
Do a restoration project				X
Go to garage sales, antique shops, and storage auctions				X
Start a scrapbook				
Raise livestock / breed small animals				X
Start a blog				X
Host a podcast				X
Create how-to videos on YouTube				X
Make a movie				X

	To Do	Doing	Done	Potential Income?
Write a book				X
Interview elders in your community				X
Learn ceramics/pottery/sculpture				X
Study interior design				X
Design/make clothing				X
Craft items for donation				
Build a point of interest				
Invent a new device				X
Find a new star				
Transfer old videos/pictures to modern media				X
Learn to play an instrument				X
Learn a new language				
Go (back) to college				
Read				
Audit college classes and lectures				
Research your genealogy				
Do brain-strengthening exercises				
Join a social club or organization				
Associate with people younger than you				
Nanny your grandkids				X
Visit friends and family				
Attend a marriage retreat				

	To Do	Doing	Done	Potential Income?
Organize a family reunion				
Create a family cookbook				X
Start a family tradition/legacy				
Go on a vacation				
Hike in an exotic location				
Visit the seven wonders of the world				
Visit the country of your ancestral origin				
Spend a year overseas				X
Go geocaching				
Go to adult summer camps				
Take river, lake, and ocean cruises				
Visit state and national parks				
Meditate				
Make a pilgrimage				
participate in mission work (domestic or international)				X
Care for the homebound or elderly				
Learn a new trade or skill				X
Volunteer at a church or nonprofit				
Volunteer to be a fund-raiser				
Coach a team				X
Write grants for organizations				X

	To Do	Doing	Done	Potential Income?
Assist a professor at a college				X
Volunteer at a library				X
Work at an animal shelter				X
Teach English (or another language) abroad				X
Teach ESL at a church or community center				X
Mentor/tutor				
Become an activist				X
Become a tour guide for your favorite place				X
Clean the environment				
Plant trees in community areas				
Deliver flowers to hospitals/ nursing homes				X
Be a candy striper at a hospital				
Work with the elderly				X
Cook and deliver meals to the homeless/elderly				
Join a theatrical group				X
Donate your clothing to local theater				
Work at election polls				X
Work on a political campaign				X
Organize a community festival				X
Volunteer at a homeless shelter and/or soup kitchen				

	To Do	Doing	Done	Potential Income?
Sign up for federal jury duty				X
Substitute teach				X
Hand out free samples at stores				X
Start a business				X
Sell arts and crafts on the Internet or at trade shows				X
Be an extra in a movie				X
Become a consultant in your former industry				X
Be a mystery shopper or product sampler				X
Start a new career				X

Made in the USA
Columbia, SC
07 January 2022

53766299R00071